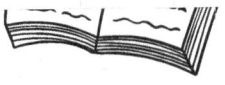

INTRODUCTION

· · · · · · · · · · · · · · · · · · · ·

Hey there! Welcome to "I Matter for Teen Boys,"
a guided journal designed for young boys like you.
Let's be honest, middle and high school can feel
like a rollercoaster ride with all its twists and turns.
From navigating changes in your body to managing
shifting friendships, academic pressures, and life's
unpredictability, it's easy to feel overwhelmed.

Throughout this journal, you will learn about yourself
by exploring your identity, expressing your emotions,
developing social skills, and learning coping skills to
overcome challenges. Think of this journal as a grow-
with-you roadmap to navigating this crazy world with
more confidence and resilience.

Remember, your voice matters, and you are unique!

I
MATTER
For Teen Boys

A Guided Journal For Teen Boys Navigating This Crazy World

Published by Diverse Children's Books Matter

ISBN: 979-8-9882977-4-1

For more information, contact:
Diverse Children's Books Matter

www.diversecbm.com
admin@nehicares.com

This Journal Belongs To:

....

Dedication

I dedicate this book to all the young boys trying to navigate this crazy world and figure out who they are. I created this journal for you to have a safe space to express yourself.

Love,

Juanita Banks-Whittington

YOU are WOrthy

Where to Start

Whether you're dealing with family issues or feeling overwhelmed by the pressures of middle or high school life, it's important to recognize that these struggles are not your fault. However, your actions may influence certain situations.

The purpose of this journal is to empower you as you grow. It will guide you towards a deeper understanding of yourself, allowing you to develop self-awareness and mindfulness. With these tools, you'll be better equipped to face challenges head-on and learn from every experience along the way.

Words of Encouragement

"The only person you should try to be
better than is the person
you were yesterday."

- Anonymous

What is Identity

Identity is who you are, what you value,
and what makes you unique.

ACTIVITY

Draw a self-portrait and write three positive qualities about yourself.

1. _____

2. _____

3. _____

BELIEVE IN YOURSELF

Words of Encouragement

"Embrace who you are and your divine purpose. Identify what you want in life and go after it with all your heart."

–Les Brown

Discovering my Identity

Discovering your identity is an ongoing journey of self-exploration. It's okay not to have all the answers right away.

Discovering my Identity

· · · · · · · · · · · · · · ·

What values and beliefs are important to you?

_____

_____

_____

_____

_____

_____

_____

_____

_____

_____

_____

_____

_____

_____

Discovering my Identity

· · · · · · · · · · · · · · · · ·

How do your beliefs and experiences shape who you are?

Discovering my Identity

· · · · · · · · · · · · · · · ·

In what ways do you express who you are?

_____

_____

_____

_____

_____

_____

_____

_____

_____

_____

_____

_____

_____

_____

_____

Discovering my Identity

. . . .

How do you express yourself beyond the
expectations others have of you?

_____

_____

_____

_____

_____

_____

_____

_____

_____

_____

_____

_____

_____

_____

_____

_____

_____

_____

Discovering my Identity

. . . .

What are some of your interests, hobbies,
or talents that make you unique?

_____

_____

_____

_____

_____

_____

_____

_____

_____

_____

_____

_____

_____

_____

_____

_____

Discovering my Identity

· · · · · · · · · · · · · · · · ·

Which qualities that make you unique do you
find most important to you and why?

ACTIVITY

Create a vision board that represents
your identity and aspirations.

GO FOR IT! 〜〜〜

DATE: _____

Dream
BIG

Words of Encouragement

" You are the author of
your own story.
Make it a great one! "

- Anonymous

★ What is Self-Esteem? ★

Self-esteem is like your personal mirror—it reflects how you view yourself, both positively and negatively. It shapes how you carry yourself, how confident you feel, and how resilient you are in facing life's twists and turns.

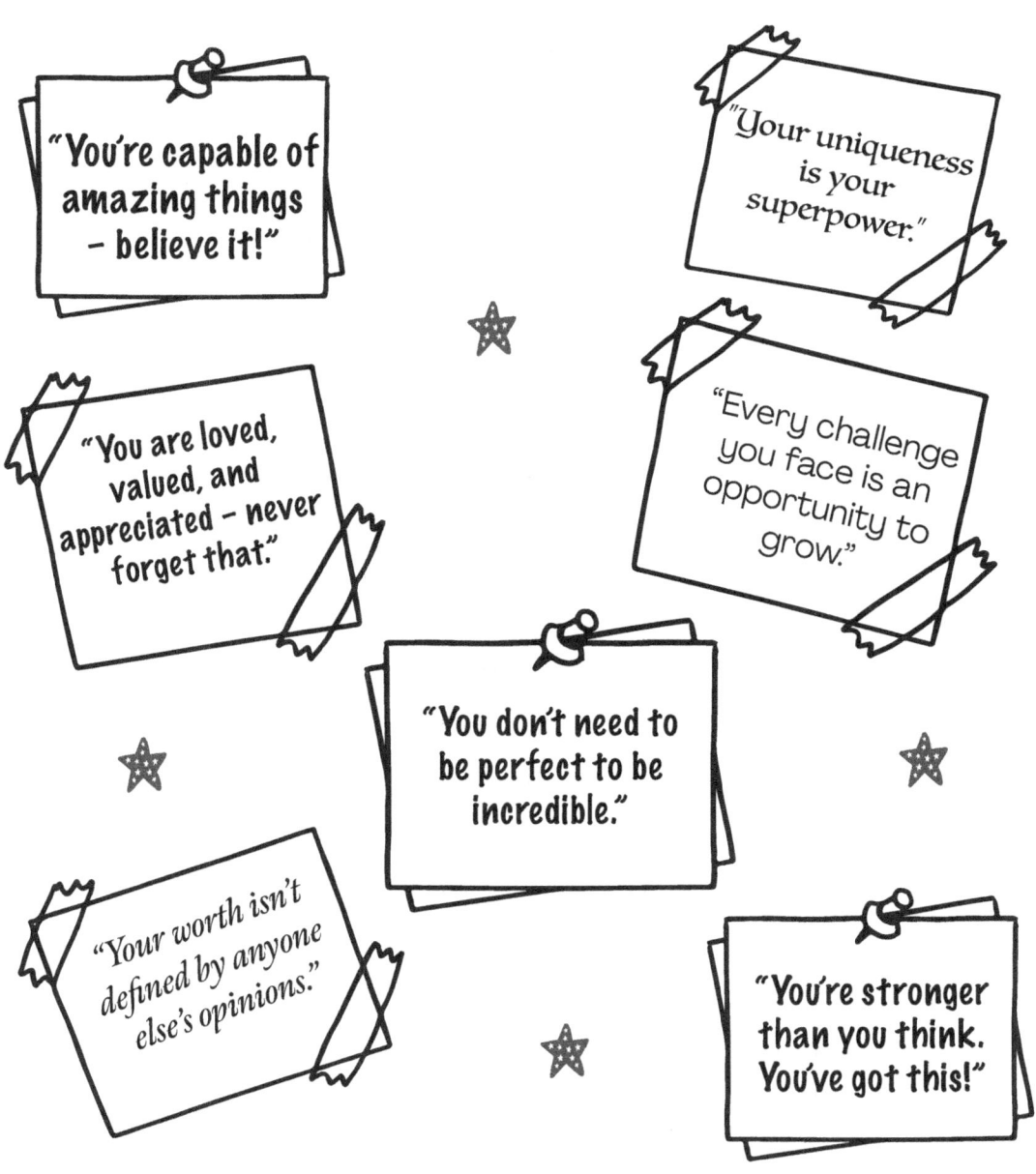

"You're capable of amazing things – believe it!"

"Your uniqueness is your superpower."

"You are loved, valued, and appreciated – never forget that."

"Every challenge you face is an opportunity to grow."

"You don't need to be perfect to be incredible."

"Your worth isn't defined by anyone else's opinions."

"You're stronger than you think. You've got this!"

Self-Esteem

. . . .

What are three things you appreciate or love about yourself that you would never change, and why?

_____

_____

_____

_____

_____

_____

_____

_____

_____

_____

_____

_____

_____

_____

_____

_____

_____

Self-Esteem

. . . .

Reflect on a time you received a compliment or accomplished something significant. How did it make you feel, and why?

Self-Esteem

. . . .

What goals and expectations have you set for yourself?
Do you think they are realistic and achievable?

Self-Esteem

. . . .

How does social media affect how you see yourself?
Have you noticed yourself comparing your life to
others online, and why?

Self-Esteem

· · · · · · · · · · · · · · · ·

What steps can you take to maintain positive
self-esteem despite external pressures, and why?
Examples: Practice self-care, confront negative
thoughts, set boundaries, and seek support.

_____

_____

_____

_____

_____

_____

_____

_____

_____

_____

_____

_____

_____

_____

Self-Esteem

How does social media affect how you see yourself?
Have you noticed yourself comparing your life to
others online, and why?

ACTIVITY

Acknowledging Your Value:
Challenge negative self-esteem by creating a list of your strengths that define your unique identity.

Creative	
	Generous
Kind	
	Forgiving
Brave	

Positive
VIBES
ONLY

Words of Encouragement

"Inhale the future, exhale the past.
Remember, in this moment,
you are enough."

- Anonymous

What are Coping Skills

Coping skills are strategies and techniques that help you manage stress, overcome challenges, and maintain your emotions.

Practice this deep breathing exercise to calm your mind and body when you're feeling stressed or anxious.

TRIANGLE
· · · · · · · · · · · · · · · ·

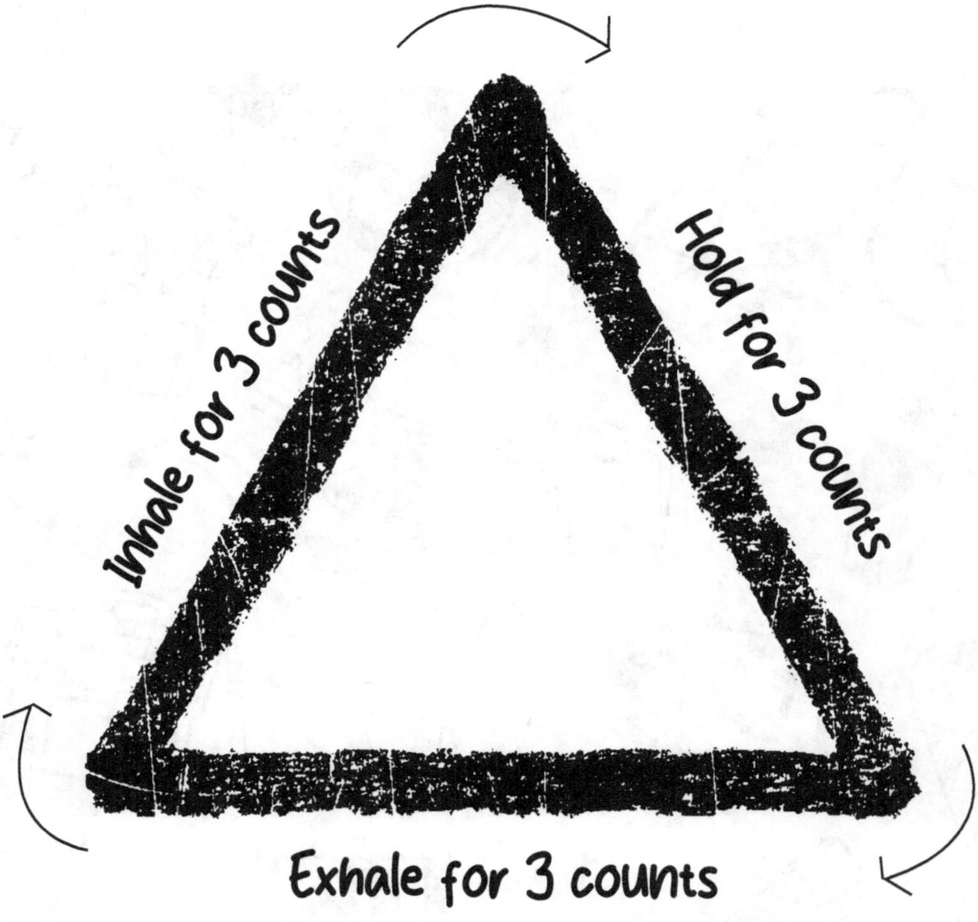

Inhale for 3 counts

Hold for 3 counts

Exhale for 3 counts

BREATHING
· · · · · · · · · · · · · · · ·

Coping Skills

· · · · · · · · · · · · · · · · ·

What are some coping skills you currently use?

Coping Skills

· · · · · · · · · · · · · · · · ·

How do you respond to stress or difficult situations?

Coping Skills

· · · · · · · · · · · · · · · ·

What are some new coping skills you would like to try?

Coping Skills

. . . .

Who is someone you can reach out to for support and comfort when you're really struggling?

ACTIVITY

Create a self-care toolkit. Fill it with items that bring you comfort and joy, such as your favorite book, a soothing playlist, stress-relief toys, and inspirational quotes. Use your toolkit whenever you need a little pick-me-up.

Words of Encouragement

"Stay true to yourself, even if it means standing alone. your health and happiness are worth protecting."

- Anonymous

⭐ What is Mindfulness? ⭐

Mindfulness is a practice of gently focusing your awareness on the present moment and being fully engaged with whatever you're doing at the moment — free from distraction or judgment.

PLANNING

POSITIVE THINKING

RELAX

MINDFULNESS

IDEA!

OPEN MIND

FORGIVE

FITNESS

YOGA

NATURE

Mindfulness

. . . .

How do you feel physically and emotionally right
now? Include any thoughts racing through
your mind at this moment.

_____

_____

_____

_____

_____

_____

_____

_____

_____

_____

_____

_____

_____

_____

_____

_____

_____

Mindfulness

· · · · · · · · · · · · · · · · ·

What activities do you currently do to help reduce your stress, worry, or regret, and why?

Mindfulness

Describe a time when being mindful helped you handle a difficult situation.

_____

_____

_____

_____

_____

_____

_____

_____

_____

_____

_____

_____

_____

_____

_____

Mindfulness

· · · · · · · · · · · · · · · ·

What mindful activities would you like to start doing to practice self-compassion or kindness towards yourself, and why? (Examples include: Deep breathing, coloring, exercising, listening to music, talking to friends, etc.)

ACTIVITY

Create a mindfulness jar and fill it with positive words or phrases. Whenever you need a boost, pick a word or phrase from the jar and reflect on its message.

Fearless

Empowered

handsome

Cheerful

TAKE CARE of You FIRST

Words of Encouragement

"Knowing yourself is the beginning of all wisdom."

- Aristotle

Setting Boundaries

· · · · · · · · · · · · · · · ·

Making responsible decisions involves considering the impact of your actions on yourself and others, weighing consequences, and prioritizing ethical considerations. It's about taking ownership of your choices and acting with integrity.

PHYSICAL  Protects your space and body, Includes sexual boundaries.

EMOTIONAL Protects your rights to have your own feelings and thoughts.

DIGITAL  Protects your privacy and communication (including texts and messages) online.

TIME  Protects how you spend your time.

FINANCIAL  Protects your financial resources and possessions.

What Boundaries Sound Like

I don't like to be called that name

I don't think that is funny

You're a little close, can you please back up?

That's not something I wish to share

Please stop

That makes me feel uncomfortable

I'll have to think about it

NO

I don't like this conversation

That hurts my feelings

I'd like to leave

This is what I need........

Setting Boundaries

· · · · · · · · · · · · · · · ·

What boundaries are most important to you and why?

Setting Boundaries

· · · · · · · · · · · · · · · · ·

What boundaries have you set with your family and friends, or you would like to set with them?

Setting Boundaries

· · · · · · · · · · · · · · · · ·

Have you ever felt your boundaries were not
valued or you didn't enforce them?
How did that make you feel?

Setting Boundaries

· · · · · · · · · · · · · · · ·

What areas of your life can use better boundary-setting: physical, emotional, time, social, etc., and why?

Setting Boundaries

· · · · · · · · · · · · · · · · · ·

Explain how you can communicate your boundaries kindly but firmly to those close to you?

ACTIVITY

Create a "Boundaries Map" where you outline your personal boundaries in different areas of your life. Practice communicating these boundaries assertively and respectfully in various situations.

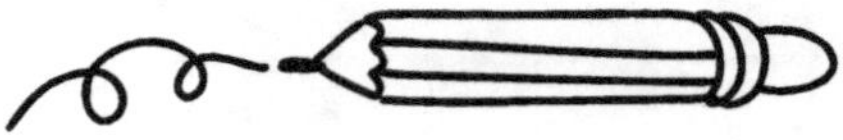

NO

It's OK To Say NO

Words of Encouragement

"The control center of your
life is your attitude."

- Anonymous

What is Self-Management

Self-management is about taking responsibility for your actions, emotions, and choices. It's about setting goals, staying focused, and practicing self-discipline to achieve success.

Self-Management

How do you handle distractions or obstacles that get in the way of your goals?

_____

_____

_____

_____

_____

_____

_____

_____

_____

_____

_____

_____

_____

_____

_____

_____

_____

Self-Management

· · · · · · · · · · · · · · · · · ·

You've had a really stressful day at school, and when you get home, you find yourself feeling frustrated and angry. What are some healthy ways you can express those intense emotions?

Self-Management

· · · · · · · · · · · · · · · · · · · ·

You're studying for a big test, but you find yourself constantly getting distracted by your phone or other things. What strategies could you use to improve your focus and concentration?

_____
_____
_____
_____
_____
_____
_____
_____
_____
_____
_____
_____
_____
_____

ACTIVITY

Imagine you have a big project due in two weeks. How would you plan and organize your time to ensure you complete the project on time without feeling overwhelmed?

To Do

This week Schedule

SAT

SUN

MON

TUE

WED

THU

FRI

S.M.A.R.T

TURNING DREAMS INTO REALITY

S **SPECIFIC**
Create a clear and specific goal.
Who, what, where and why?

M **MEASURABLE**
You can't improve what you can't measure.
How will you track your goal?

A **ACHIEVABLE**
Create a goal that is challenging but not impossible.
Are you aiming too high or low?

R **RELEVANT**
Keep your goal realistic.
Be honest, what are you capable of?

T **TIME FRAME**
A date to keep you accountable.
What do you need to complete by certain dates?

Here's an example to guide you in creating your own SMART Goal:

1. Goal: Submitting All my Assignments on Time

S   I will ensure I complete and submit all my assignments by their designated deadlines.

M   I will track assignments and due dates using a physical and digital checklist, promptly checking off each task once it is completed and turned in.

A   I will divide larger tasks into smaller, manageable parts and schedule them with specific deadlines to ensure timely accomplishment.

R   Submitting assignments promptly is essential for maintaining my academic performance, displaying responsibility, and showing dedication to success.

T   By the end of the semester, my goal is to have no more than two late assignment submissions to any teacher.

ACTIVITY

Set 2 goals for yourself (academic, personal, or social) and outline steps to achieve them.

1. Goal: _____

S ....

....

M ....

....

A ....

....

R ....

....

T ....

....

MY smart GOALS ARE:

· · · · · · · · · · · · · · · · · · ·

2. Goal: _____

S

M

A

R

T

Words of Encouragement

"Empathy is seeing with the eyes of
another, listening with the ears
of another, and feeling with
the heart of another."

- Alfred Adler

What is Social Awareness

Social awareness involves understanding and empathizing with others, including those from different backgrounds or cultures. It's about recognizing and respecting diversity, building meaningful connections, and acting ethically in your interactions.

Social Awareness

· · · · · · · · · · · · · · · ·

How do you educate yourself about social issues
and current events?

Social Awareness

You notice a classmate sitting alone during lunch, looking upset. What could you do or say to let them know you care about their feelings?

_____

_____

_____

_____

_____

_____

_____

_____

_____

_____

_____

_____

_____

Social Awareness

You overhear someone making an insensitive comment about another person's culture or background. What would be a thoughtful way to address the situation and promote understanding?

Social Awareness

· · · · · · · · · · · · · · · ·

Have you ever experienced a situation where
you felt misunderstood or left out?
How did it make you feel?

_____

_____

_____

_____

_____

_____

_____

_____

_____

_____

_____

_____

_____

_____

_____

ACTIVITY

Describe a social issue you are passionate about. List three things you could do at school or with peers to use your voice and advocate for positive social change.

....

....

....

....

1. _____

2. _____

3. _____

Turn
Challenges
INTO
Opportunities

Words of Encouragement

"The quality of your relationships determines the quality of your life."

- Esther Perel

What are Relationship Skills

· · · · · · · · · · · · · · · · ·

Relationship skills are essential for building and maintaining healthy connections with others. These skills include effective communication, conflict resolution, and knowing when to offer support or seek help.

Relationship Skills

· · · · · · · · · · · · · · · · ·

What qualities do you value most in a close
friend, and why?

_____

_____

_____

_____

_____

_____

_____

_____

_____

_____

_____

_____

_____

_____

_____

_____

_____

_____

Relationship Skills

· · · · · · · · · · · · · · · · ·

How do you demonstrate those same qualities
yourself when building and maintaining friendships?

Relationship Skills

· · · · · · · · · · · · · · · ·

Think about a time when you had a disagreement or
conflict with a friend or family member.
How did you handle the situation?

_____

_____

_____

_____

_____

_____

_____

_____

_____

_____

_____

_____

_____

_____

_____

_____

Relationship Skills

• • • • • • • • • • • • • • • • •

In that situation, what could you have done differently to communicate more effectively or resolve the conflict in a healthier way?

_____

_____

_____

_____

_____

_____

_____

_____

_____

_____

_____

_____

_____

_____

_____

Relationship Skills

· · · · · · · · · · · · · · ·

What has helped you form positive relationships in the past?

Relationship Skills

· · · · · · · · · · · · · · · · ·

How do you show appreciation and support
for the people you care about?

 **ACTIVITY**

Write an appreciation letter to someone who has had a positive impact on your life. You can choose to share it with them or reflect on what you think their response would be here.

_____

_____

_____

_____

_____

_____

_____

_____

_____

_____

_____

_____

BUILD

Bridges Of

Understanding

Words of Encouragement

"The best way to predict the future is to create it."

- Abraham Lincoln

Making Responsible Decisions

Making responsible decisions involves considering the impact of your actions on yourself and others, weighing consequences, and prioritizing ethical considerations. It's about taking ownership of your choices and acting with integrity.

Making Responsible Decisions

. . . .

What role do your values and beliefs play in when making decisions?

Making Responsible Decisions

· · · · · · · · · · · · · · · ·

What do you consider when making
important choices or decisions, and why?

Making Responsible Decisions

. . . .

You have an important test coming up, but your friends invite you to hang out. How would you decide what to do in this situation, and why?

Making Responsible Decisions

If you notice a friend engaging in behavior that could be harmful to themselves or others, such as bullying or substance abuse. What would you consider when deciding whether to intervene, and how would you do it?

ACTIVITY

Fill out the decision-making wheel to help you make responsible choices in different situations.

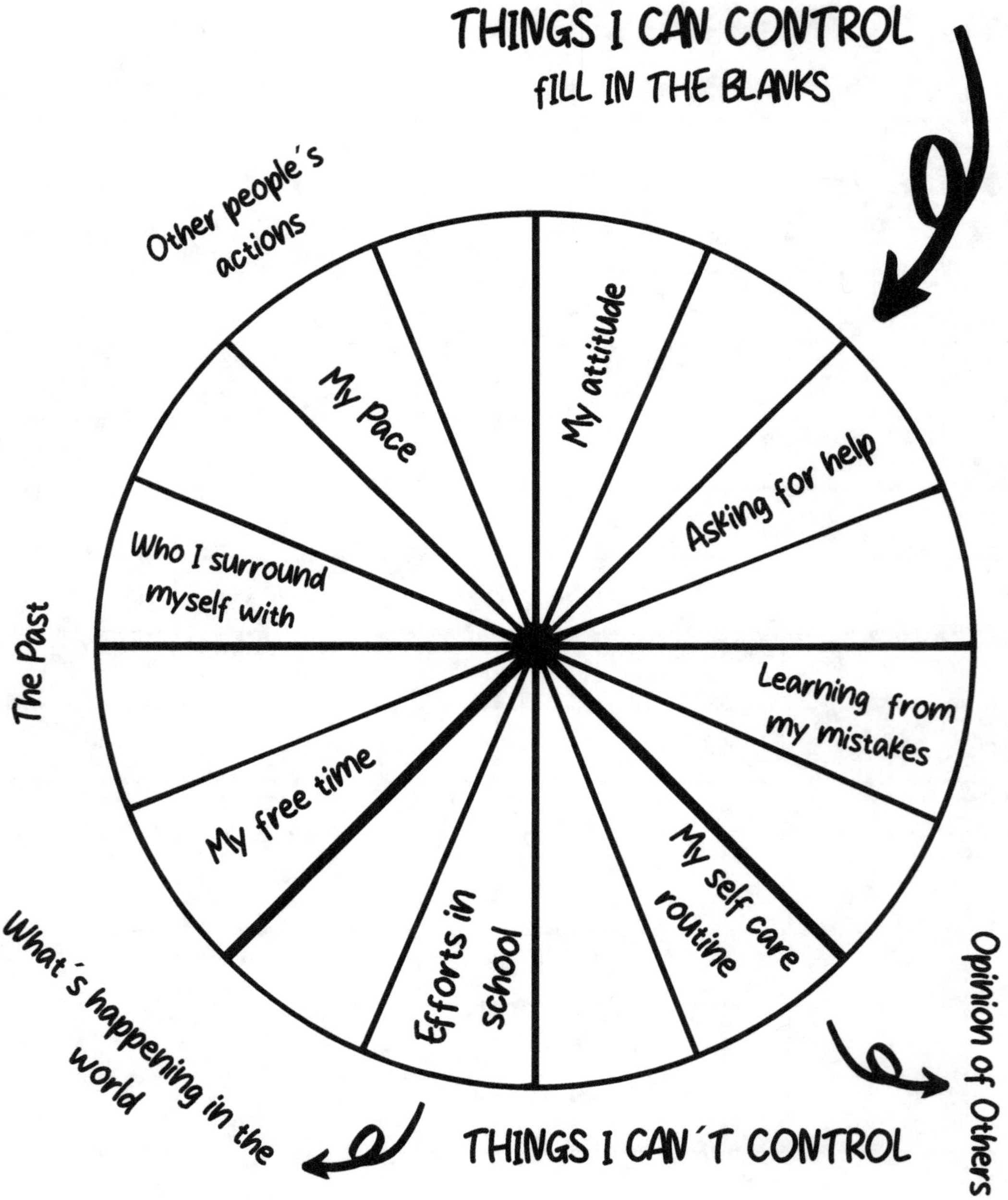

THINGS I CAN CONTROL
FILL IN THE BLANKS

- Other people's actions
- My Pace
- My attitude
- Asking for help
- Who I surround myself with
- The Past
- Learning from my mistakes
- My free time
- Efforts in school
- My self care routine
- What's happening in the world
- Opinion of Others

THINGS I CAN'T CONTROL

92

EVERYTHING will be OK

Words of Encouragement

"Confidence isn't about knowing you'll succeed; it's about trusting yourself even when you don't."

– Anonymous

What is Confidence

Confidence is all about believing in yourself and what you can do. When you're confident, you will face challenges with a strong sense of self-belief, bounce back from setbacks, maintain a positive attitude, pursue your goals, and handle whatever life throws your way.

Confidence

Confidence starts with believing in yourself. It's about recognizing your strengths, talents, and unique qualities. When do you feel most confident about yourself and why?

_____

_____

_____

_____

_____

_____

_____

_____

_____

_____

_____

_____

_____

_____

_____

Confidence

Confidence is linked to how you see yourself. It's about having a positive self-image and feeling good about who you are, both inside and out. How do you increase your confidence when you're feeling unsure or insecure?

_____

_____

_____

_____

_____

_____

_____

_____

_____

_____

_____

_____

Confidence

Whether it's trying out for a sports team, speaking up in class, or pursuing a new hobby, confidence enables you to embrace new experiences and grow as a person. Have you ever let fear of failure hold you back from pursuing something you were passionate about?

_____

_____

_____

_____

_____

_____

_____

_____

_____

_____

_____

_____

_____

_____

Confidence

· · · · · · · · · · · · · · · ·

Confidence doesn't mean you'll never face challenges or setbacks. It's about learning and growing from experiences when things don't go as planned. How did you overcome the fear of failure you experienced in the previous situation?

_____

_____

_____

_____

_____

_____

_____

_____

_____

_____

_____

_____

_____

Using Affirmations to Build My Confidence

Affirmations are positive statements you repeat to yourself to challenge negative thoughts and beliefs.

I am smart, strong, and capable of achieving anything I set my mind to.

My strengths and weaknesses make me who I am.

I ACCEPT MYSELF

I AM BRAVE

TODAY I CHOOSE ME

REMEMBER WHO YOU TRULY ARE

I DESERVE HAPINESS

I am loved and matter.

 **ACTIVITY**

Create a "Confidence Boost" list by writing
affirmations on the mirror to challenge
any negative thoughts or beliefs about
yourself to encourage positive thoughts.

LOVE
YOU

Natural
Wax

Words of Encouragement

"Character is not defined by what you say but by what you do. Let your actions reflect the goodness within your heart."

– Steve Maraboli

 # What is Character

Character is the qualities that makeup who you are as a person and guide your thoughts, actions, and decisions.

Integrity

SECRETIVE

Adventurous

Silly

COURAGEOUS

Wise

respect

Energetic

Quiet

SERIOUS

cheerful

Focused

RUDE

Joyful

fearless

Helpful

dependable

friendly

Humble

CONSIDERATE

compassionate

intelligent

Honest

Moody

Trustworthy

courteous

Aggressive

Selfish

Caring

Brave

agreeable

Negative

Character

. . . .

What character traits are most important to you and why?

Character

How do your character traits
guide your actions and decisions?

Character

· · · · · · · · · · · · · · · ·

How do you show kindness, honesty,
and compassion in your interactions with others?

Character

Have you ever faced a situation that tested your
character or integrity? How did you respond?

Write down three personal character traits that mean the most to you and why. Display them somewhere you can see them every day outside of your journal.

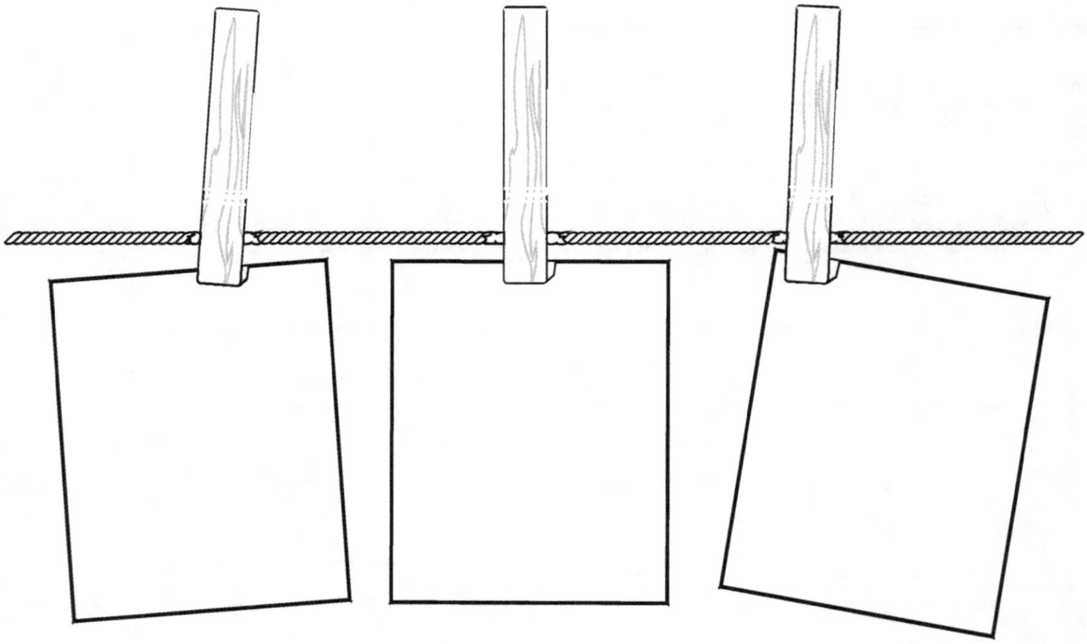

Stay CURIOUS, Keep Exploring YOU

Words of Encouragement

"Stay true to yourself, even if it means standing alone. Your health and happiness are worth protecting."

- Anonymous

Peer Pressure and Making Positive Choices

. . . .

Peer pressure is when your friends or peers influence your decisions. Making positive choices that align with your values and goals is important.

Peer Pressure and Making Positive Choices

. . . .

What is your definition of peer pressure and how has it influenced your life?

_____

_____

_____

_____

_____

_____

_____

_____

_____

_____

_____

_____

_____

_____

Peer Pressure and Making Positive Choices

. . . .

Share a situation when you felt pressured to do something you didn't want to do. How did you handle the situation?

Peer Pressure and Making Positive Choices

· · · · · · · · · · · · · · · · · ·

How did you handle the pressure?

_____

_____

_____

_____

_____

_____

_____

_____

_____

_____

_____

_____

_____

Peer Pressure and Making Positive Choices

....

What do you do to resist peer pressure and make positive choices?

Making a Positive Choices Plan

Use this example to help you create
a Positive Choices Plan.

Goal: Improve my grades by one letter grade in all subjects by the end of the semester.

Potential Challenges:

1.
Procrastination and time management issues.

2.
Difficulty understanding certain subjects or topics.

3.
Distractions from social media or other activities.

Strategies for Overcoming Challenges:

1.
Set specific study schedules and use a planner to manage time effectively.

2.
Seek help from teachers, tutors, or classmates when struggling with difficult concepts.

3.
Limit social media usage during study sessions and utilize apps or website blockers if necessary.

ACTIVITY

Create a "Positive Choices Plan" where you identify three goals for making positive choices in different areas of your life. Include potential challenges and strategies for overcoming them.

Goal:

Potential Challenges:

1.

2.

3.

Strategies for Overcoming Challenges:

1.

2.

3.

Goal:

Potential Challenges:

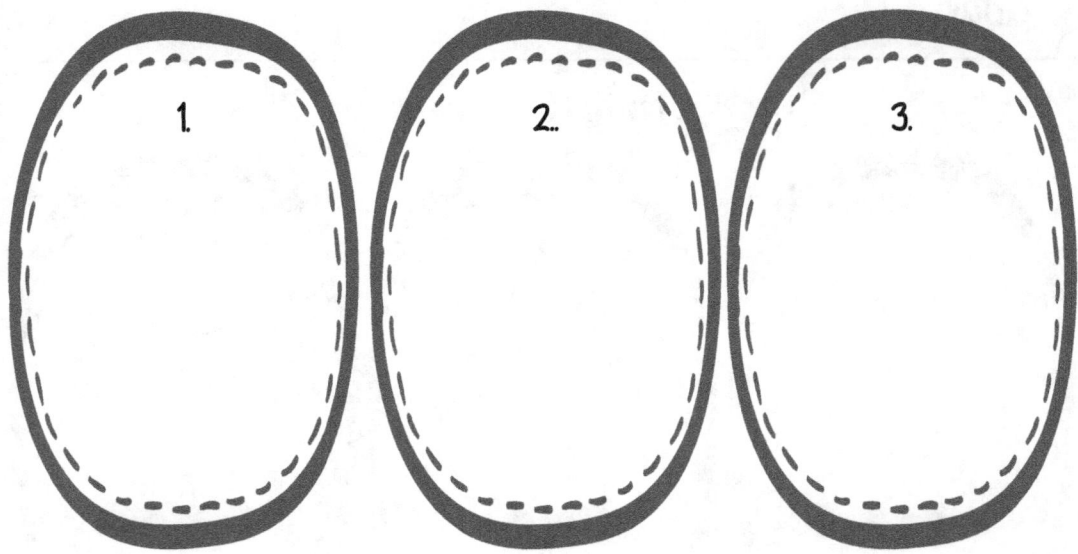

1. 2. 3.

Strategies for Overcoming Challenges:

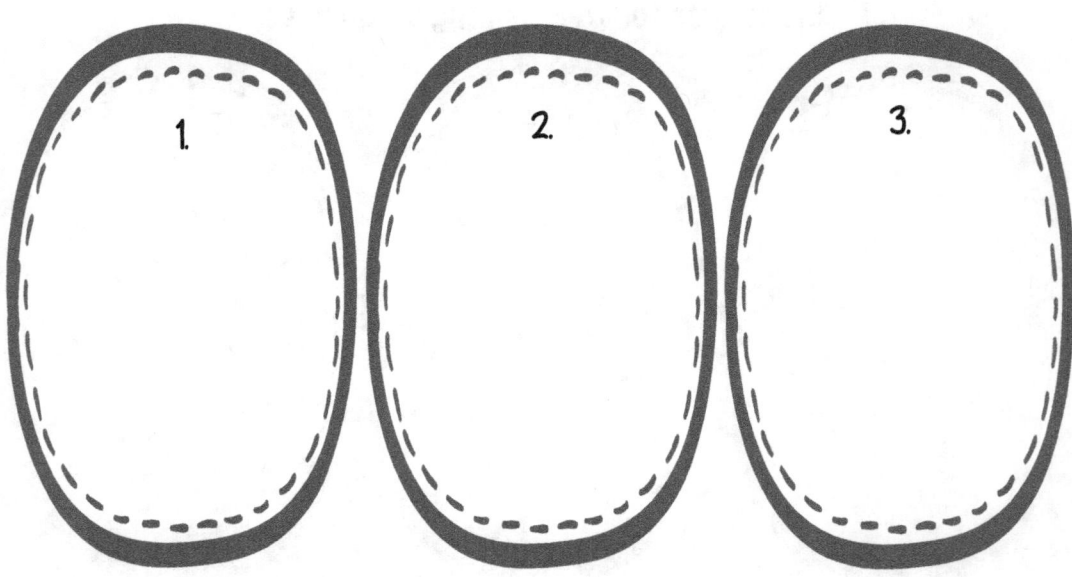

1. 2. 3.

Be The CHANGE You Wish To See In The WORLD

Words of Encouragement

"Family is important, but so is staying true to yourself. Find the courage to pursue your own dreams, even if they differ from what others expect of you."

- Anonymous

Family Expectations

Family expectations are the beliefs, behaviors, and values your family may have for you from an early age. While respecting your family's values and traditions is important, it's also okay to have your own dreams and aspirations.

Respect

Academic Success   OPENLY COMMUNICATES   Leader

Curiosity   Time Management   Attend School

Honesty

SELF-CONTROL   Responsible   Avoids Distractions

Trustworthy   Self-discipline   Independent

Sets & Completes Goal   Integrity   EMPATHIC COMPASSIONATE

Flexible   Personal Growth   Social Skills

Positive Relationships   Prioritizes Health

Financial Awareness   Resolves Conflict Peaceful   Truthful

Authentic   Community Service

Family Expectations

What expectations or pressures does your family
have for you? How do they impact
your choices and goals?

_____

_____

_____

_____

_____

_____

_____

_____

_____

_____

_____

_____

_____

_____

Family Expectations

Have you ever felt conflicted between following your family's expectations and pursuing your own dreams? How did you handle this challenge?

Family Expectations

How do you communicate with your family about their expectations of you?

_____

_____

_____

_____

_____

_____

_____

_____

_____

_____

_____

_____

_____

_____

_____

_____

_____

Family Expectations

How can you communicate with your family about your needs and goals even if it's a hard discussion?

_____
_____
_____
_____
_____
_____
_____
_____
_____
_____
_____
_____
_____
_____
_____
_____

Family Expectations

What boundaries do you or can you set to maintain a healthy balance between honoring your family's expectations and staying true to who you are?

ACTIVITY

· · · · · · · · · · · · · · · ·

Create a family expectations chart to compare and reflect on which expectations feel supportive and restrictive.

	Family Expectations	My Expectations
Career or Educational Paths		
Academic Success		
Cultural Traditions		
Responsibilities at Home		
Family Values		
Personal Behavior		

Words of Encouragement

"Be yourself; everyone
else is already taken."

- Oscar Wilde

Expressing Myself on Social Media

Social media is an outlet for self-expression and connecting with others who share similar experiences and interests. It also comes with risks and challenges, so important to be mindful of what you post.

Expressing Myself on Social Media

Which social media platforms do you use
to express yourself and connect with others?
Do you share thoughts, photos, artwork,
or other forms of creative expression?

_____

_____

_____

_____

_____

_____

_____

_____

_____

_____

_____

_____

Expressing Myself
on Social Media

· · · · · · · · · · · · · · · · ·

Do you have any topics or parts of your life
that you prefer to keep private when it
comes to social media and why?

Expressing Myself
on Social Media

· · · · · · · · · · · · · · · · ·

Have you ever felt pressured to portray a specific image or persona on social media? How did you deal with this pressure?

_____

_____

_____

_____

_____

_____

_____

_____

_____

_____

_____

_____

_____

Expressing Myself
on Social Media

Have you experienced cyberbullying or negative interactions on social media? How did you respond?

Expressing Myself
on Social Media

What boundaries do you set for yourself when using social media to protect your privacy, authenticity, mental and emotional health?

1. On your social media or this cell phone, share a photo or artwork representing something meaningful to you and write a caption explaining why.

2. Write a supportive comment on someone else's post or this cell phone to spread kindness and encouragement.

Words of Encouragement

"Mentorship is a journey of shared learning and growth. Be open to both giving and receiving guidance, and embrace the transformative power of mentorship."

– Anonymous

The Power of Mentorship

Mentorship is a valuable resource that can provide guidance, support, and inspiration you as you navigate through life's challenges and opportunities. Having a mentor allows you to learn from someone with more experience and wisdom, helping you develop essential skills and perspectives for personal and professional growth.

The Power of Mentorship

Have you ever had a mentor or role model who inspired you? What specific qualities did they have that you found admirable?

The Power of Mentorship

Who are some mentors, icons, or elders that you admire? What qualities do you value in them?

The Power of Mentorship

What qualities do you think are important for a mentor to have, and why?

The Power of Mentorship

Which areas of your life do you think could benefit with the added support and insights from a mentor?

Contacting a Potential Mentor

. . . .

Use the following template as a helpful guide:

Hello [Potential Mentor's Name],

I am [Your Name], a [Your Grade] student at [Your School]. I'm actively involved in [club/extracurricular activity], and passionate about learning more about [a specific skill/subject].

I've been inspired by your impressive achievements, expertise, and commitment to [mention something specific that you admire about your potential mentor].

I would be honored to have you as my mentor as I navigate who I am. Learning and receiving guidance from you will help me nurture my [mention your area of interest or career aspirations].

Thank you for considering my request. I look forward to hearing from you and hope we can work together to enhance my skills and achieve my goals.

Sincerely,
[Your Name]

ACTIVITY

Utilize the provided template to draft a letter to someone you admire and ask them to be your mentor.

Words of Encouragement

"If you don't love yourself, nobody will.
Not only that, you won't be
good at loving anyone else.
Loving starts with the self."

- Wayne Dyer

What is Self-Care

· · · · · · · · · · · · · · · · ·

Self-care involves intentionally taking time to prioritize your physical, emotional, and mental health. It's about recognizing and honoring your own and making choices that promote health and happiness.

Tips to Enhance
Physical Self-Care

· ·

✦ Ensure you get enough sleep each night (8-10 hours).

✦ Maintain a balanced diet rich in fruits, vegetables, lean proteins, whole grains, and drink water.

✦ Stay active with regular physical activities like walking, jogging, dancing, or sports.

✦ Maintain good hygiene habits by showering regularly, brushing your teeth, and washing your hands.

Tips to Enhance
Emotional Self-Care

- ✦ Recognize and accept your emotions without criticism.

- ✦ Share your feelings through writing, art, or confiding in a trusted individual.

- ✦ Establish boundaries to safeguard your emotional health when interacting with others.

- ✦ Show yourself self-compassion or grace by being kind and empathetic towards yourself.

Tips to Enhance
Mental Self-Care

· ·

Give your mind a break by stepping away from screens and technology.

Engage in activities that boost your creativity and mental stimulation like reading, puzzles, or picking up a new skill.

Practice mindfulness or meditation to quiet your mind and reduce stress.

Combat negative thoughts with positive self-talk and affirmations.

LEARN
And
GROW

Tips to Enhance
Social Self-Care

∙∙∙∙∙∙∙∙∙∙∙∙∙∙∙∙∙∙∙∙∙∙∙∙

Surround yourself with friends and family who inspire and encourage you.

Engage in social activities that bring happiness and satisfaction.

Establish healthy boundaries in relationships and make time for self-care.

Participate in clubs, groups, or organizations that resonate with your passions and beliefs.

Tips to Improving Gratitude

· ·

Participate in activities that improve your gratitude like journaling, meditation, setting boundaries, and practicing self-compassion.

Reflect on your values, beliefs, and purpose in life.

Connect with a supportive community or mentor who aligns with your beliefs.

Incorporate gratitude and concentrate on the parts of your life that bring you happiness and satisfaction.

Tips for Improving Self-Discipline

· ·

⭐ Prioritize your commitments and responsibilities to prevent feeling overwhelmed.

⚡ Practice saying no to activities or obligations that consume your time or energy.

👑 Incorporate regular breaks and downtime to relax and rejuvenate.

✈ Establish achievable goals and acknowledge your accomplishments, no matter how big or small.

⭐

CREATE CHANGE

Words of Encouragement

"The only way to make sense out of change is to plunge into it, move with it, and join the dance."

- Alan Watts

"Reflection is the key to growth and transformation. Embrace the journey of self-discovery and continue to evolve into the best version of yourself."

- Anonymous

Reflection and Moving Forward

Reflection is taking time to look back on your journey, acknowledge your growth, learn from mistakes, and set future goals.

MY GROWTH MATTERS

Reflection and Moving Forward

· ·

What valuable lessons or insights have you learned
from completing this journal?

_____

_____

_____

_____

_____

_____

_____

_____

_____

_____

_____

_____

_____

_____

_____

_____

Reflection and Moving Forward

· ·

What has been the biggest "aha!" moment you experienced from this journal?

_____
_____
_____
_____
_____
_____
_____
_____
_____
_____
_____
_____
_____
_____
_____

Reflection and Moving Forward

· ·

How have your attitudes, beliefs, or behaviors
changed due to your reflections?

_____

_____

_____

_____

_____

_____

_____

_____

_____

_____

_____

_____

_____

_____

Reflection and Moving Forward

· ·

What challenges are you still facing regarding your identity, goals or purpose? Why do you think you are still facing these challenges?

_____

_____

_____

_____

_____

_____

_____

_____

_____

_____

_____

_____

_____

_____

_____

Reflection and Moving Forward

....

How will you incorporate self-reflection into your daily life moving forward?

ACTIVITY

Create a self-care checklist with at least three goals you would like to work on in the next 30 days, with affirmations to help you achieve them.

 Self-Care

My Mind's Goals	Daily Affirmation
○	
○	
○	
○	
○	
○	
○	

YES,

YOU

MATTER!

 Conclusion

Congratulations on completing
"I Matter For Teen Boys,"
A Guided Journal For Young Boys Navigating
This Crazy World! Remember, your voice matters.
You deserve love, support, and happiness. Keep
exploring, growing, and believing in yourself. You
can create a bright future for yourself, no matter
what challenges you may face.

Keep shining bright!

9 789898 829774 1